I Love Ewe

An Ode to Animal Moms

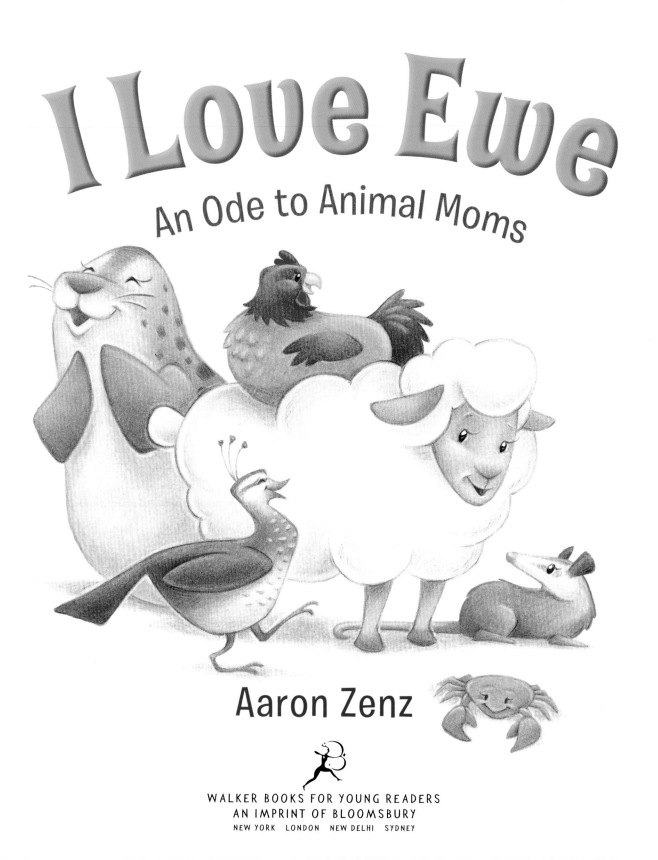

Aaron Zenz

WALKER BOOKS FOR YOUNG READERS
AN IMPRINT OF BLOOMSBURY
NEW YORK   LONDON   NEW DELHI   SYDNEY

For *my* mom, **Sue Zenz**—
a real hoot and a half

First published in the United States of America in March 2013
by Walker Books for Young Readers. an imprint of Bloomsbury Publishing. Inc.
www.bloomsburykids.com

For information about permission to reproduce selections from this book. write to
Permissions. Walker BFYR. 175 Fifth Avenue. New York. New York 10010

Library of Congress Cataloging-in-Publication Data
Zenz. Aaron.
I love ewe : an ode to animal moms / by Aaron Zenz.
p.   cm.
Summary: From baby geese to kangaroos to humans. every mom and dad is known by his or her own
special name. Bouncing texts full of fun wordplay and adorable illustrations feature animal parents of every
shape and size. and encourage little readers to express big love. Don't be afraid to say I love ewe!
ISBN 978-0-8027-2826-5 (hardcover) • ISBN 978-0-8027-2827-2 (reinforced)
[1. Stories in rhyme. 2. Animals—Nomenclature—Fiction.] I. Title.
PZ8.3.Z42Iaal 2013   [E]—dc23   2012020806

Art created with 44 Prismacolor colored pencils (and 95 broken pencil tips)
Typeset in Arbitrary Regular and Shag Expert Exotica
Book design by Nicole Gastonguay

Printed in China by C&C Offset Printing Co.. Ltd.. Shenzhen. Guangdong
2 4 6 8 10 9 7 5 3 1 (hardcover)
2 4 6 8 10 9 7 5 3 1 (reinforced)

My mom's a **COW**—I bet you knew that.

But did you know
not all **COWS** moo?

My mom's a **HEN**—

But look again . . .

HENS live underwater too!

Mommy is a hootin' **NANNY**.

Mommy is the **QUEEN** of clean.

SOW

is how

we name

our

mommies,

big or small or in between.

We like hanging with our mothers.
If you called them, you'd address

a **LIONESS**,

a **PANTHERESS**,

a **TIGRESS**, and

a **LEOPARDESS**.

Mama is a happy **PEAHEN**.

Ma's a **VIXEN**.

Ma's a
MARE.

Mama is a frequent **FLYER**—

see us leaping through the *air!*

Our moms' names are **JILL** and **JENNY**.

Does *your* mom have her own name too?

There's no other **PEN** pal like her!

DOE . . . you love me?

Oh, I love **EWE**.

BEAR — SOW
CAT — QUEEN
CHICKEN — HEN
COW — COW

CRAB — HEN
DEER — DOE
DONKEY — JENNY
ELEPHANT — COW
FOX — VIXEN

GOAT — NANNY
HIPPOPOTAMUS — COW
HORSE — MARE
KANGAROO — FLYER

LEOPARD — LEOPARDESS
LION — LIONESS
LOBSTER — HEN
MOLE — SOW
OCTOPUS — HEN

OPOSSUM — JILL
PANTHER — PANTHERESS
PEAFOWL — PEAHEN
PIG — SOW

RHINOCEROS — COW
SEAL — COW
SHEEP — EWE
SWAN — PEN
TIGER — TIGRESS